Amazing Animal Hunters

EAGLES

by Sally Morgan

amicus

Published by Amicus
P.O. Box 1329, Mankato, Minnesota 56002

Printed in the United States of America at Corporate Graphics, in North Mankato, Minnesota.

Library of Congress Cataloging-in-Publication Data
Morgan, Sally.
  Eagles / by Sally Morgan.
     p. cm. -- (Amazing animal hunters)
  Includes index.
  Summary: "Discusses the life of eagles and profiles different types of eagles,
along with providing facts about food, shelter, habitat, and more. Also includes
records on eagles"--Provided by publisher.
  ISBN 978-1-60753-045-9 (library binding)
  1. Eagles--Juvenile literature. I. Title.
  QL696.F32M657 2011
  598.9'42--dc22

                                                       2009048512

Created by Q2AMedia
Editor: Katie Dicker
Art Director: Harleen Mehta
Designer: Tarang Saggar
Picture Researcher: Sujatha Menon

All words in **bold** can be found in the Glossary on pages 30–31.

Picture credits
t=top b=bottom c=center l=left r=right
Cover images: Fritz Poelking/Photolibrary, Vulnificans/Shutterstock

Open Best Design Stock/Shutterstock: Title page, Sam Dcrz/Shutterstock: Contents page, Fritz Polking/Ecoscene: 4,
Dirkr/Shutterstock: 5t, Michael/Bigstockphoto: 5b, Bernd Zoller/Photolibrary: 6, Heinz Plenge/Photolibrary: 7t, SJ. Krasemann/
Photolibrary: 7b, Patricio Robles Gil/Photolibrary: 8, Morales Morales/Photolibrary: 9l, PLoS Biology: 9r, Steven Kazlowski/
Ecoscene: 10, Steven Kazlowski/Photolibrary: 11, Pavel Aleynikov/Dreamstime: 12, FloridaStock/Istockphoto: 13t,
Johan Swanepoel/Istockphoto: 13b, Frank Greenaway/Getty Images: 14, Berndt Fischer/Photolibrary: 15t, Joel Sartore/
Getty Images: 15b, Fritz Polking/Ecoscene: 16, Peter Cairns/Ecoscene: 17t, Martin Harvey/Corbis: 17b, Mark Hamblin/
Photolibrary: 18, Istockphoto: 19t, Vincent Munier/Nature Picture Library: 19b, Fritz Polking/Ecoscene: 20, Roland Mayr/
Photolibrary: 21, Dr Peter Wernicke/Photolibrary: 22, Fritz Polking/Ecoscene; 23, Juan Manuel Renjifo/Photolibrary: 24,
Joel Bennett/Photolibrary: 25t, Tim Laman/Getty Images: 25b, Alfredo Maiquez/Photolibrary: 26, Peter Oxford/Nature Picture
Library: 27l, Ricardo Azoury/Istockphoto: 27r, Patricio Robles Gil/Photolibrary: 28, Prague Modrany/Istockphoto: 29,
Johan Swanepoel/Istockphoto: 31.

DAD0043
42010

9 8 7 6 5 4 3 2 1

Contents

King of the Birds

Swooping down from above is a huge bird. As it stretches out its talons, it grabs a scurrying rabbit from the ground. It is an eagle, one of the most powerful birds on Earth.

Bird of Prey

Eagles are "birds of prey" that hunt other animals. They are related to hawks and vultures. There are about 60 different **species** (or types) of eagle in the world. The largest is the Philippine eagle, with a massive wingspan of more than 6.5 feet (2 m). The smallest is the ornate hawk-eagle, with wings just under 4 feet (1.2 m) across. Eagles are divided into four groups—booted eagles, fish or sea eagles, buzzard eagles, and snake eagles.

The word eagle comes from the Latin word *Aquila,* the name given to the golden eagle by the Romans. This magnificent bird is a sea eagle.

Sharp claws called talons

This sea eagle has a white tail

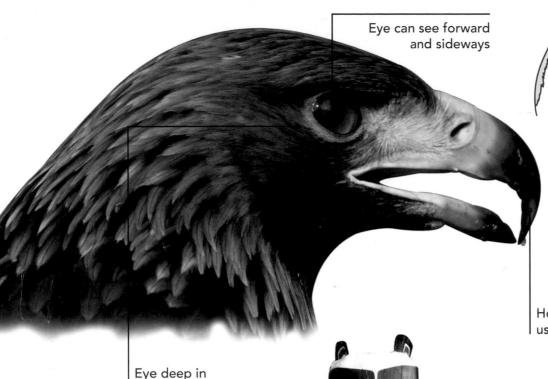

Eye can see forward and sideways

Eagles have excellent eyesight and powerful beaks.

Eye deep in socket

Hooked beak used for hunting

Sacred Birds

These wonderful birds play an important role in the culture of many countries. In North America, the eagle is sacred to some **Native** Americans. The feathers are used in ceremonies and given to people to mark their bravery or other achievements. In Peru, the eagle is worshipped as an animal god. Eagles are seen as a symbol of power, strength, and courage. The Romans chose the eagle as their emblem, and today the eagle is found on the **coat of arms** of countries such as Germany, Poland, and Egypt. The bald eagle is also the national symbol of the United States.

A totem pole tells a story, and eagles are often carved at the top.

SUN WORSHIP

In ancient times, the sun was worshipped as a god in parts of South America. People thought that the eagle was a messenger of the sun god.

5

Deadly Predators

Eagles are expert hunters, well equipped with weapons—a hooked beak and razor-sharp claws, called talons. They hunt for food while they are flying, using their excellent vision to spot **prey**.

Body of a Hunter

The eagle has the perfect body for hunting. It is covered in feathers, which form a smooth surface that slips easily and quickly through the air. Their massive feet end in huge curved talons, which they use to catch, grip, and kill their prey. When an eagle catches a creature, it uses its sharp talons to pierce the flesh and to crush the bones. It also uses the sharp-edged hook on its large beak to rip the animal to pieces.

An eagle has no trouble catching a slippery fish, using its sharp talons.

Leg covered
in scales

Toes end in curved
claws or talons

Three forward-pointing toes and
one backward-pointing toe

The talons of the harpy
eagle are the size of a
tiger's claws. They crush
the bones of their prey.

Incredible Sight

Eagles have very large eyes in comparison to the
size of their head. As day-time hunters, sight is their
most important sense. They use their eyes to see
forward and to the side of their head at the same
time, giving them good all-around vision. Eagles see
in color, as humans do, but they also see in infrared
and ultraviolet light, which are invisible to people.
They help the eagle spot **camouflaged** prey on
the ground and fish swimming in water.

EAGLE EYES

Eagles can see far
more detail than we
can. In fact, scientists
think that an eagle
may be able to spot
a rabbit on the ground
from a distance of
a mile (1.6 km).

Eagle Homes

Eagles are powerful fliers. They can travel long distances, so they are found around the world. The only places where eagles are not found today are New Zealand, a few remote islands in the Pacific Ocean, and the Antarctic.

Where Do Eagles Live?

Eagles live in many different **habitats**, from **tropical jungles** to the frozen Arctic. Golden eagles are seen gliding high over mountains, while bateleurs and snake eagles hunt over tropical grasslands in Africa. The steppe eagle prefers the cooler grasslands of Central Asia. Harpy eagles are found in the jungles of South America. Sea eagles feed on fish, so they stay close to coasts, rivers, and lakes. Some eagles are even found **scavenging** in garbage dumps, or nesting on tall buildings in towns and cities.

This eagle, called the ornate hawk-eagle, lives in the forests of Mexico.

Long-Distance Travel

Some eagles make regular journeys, called **migrations**. In fall, when rivers and lakes start to freeze over, bald eagles living in the northern parts of North America migrate south. They fly to the coast, or to wetlands where it is warmer and there is plenty of food. The Steller's sea eagle of eastern Russia flies south to Japan, a distance of about 1,243 miles (2,000 km), and travels more than 93 miles (150 km) on each day of its journey.

BIG BIRD

The largest ever eagle was the giant Haast's eagle (below), which is now **extinct**. It used to live in New Zealand where it preyed on the moa, a large flightless bird that is also extinct. The moa was up to 15 times heavier than the Haast's eagle!

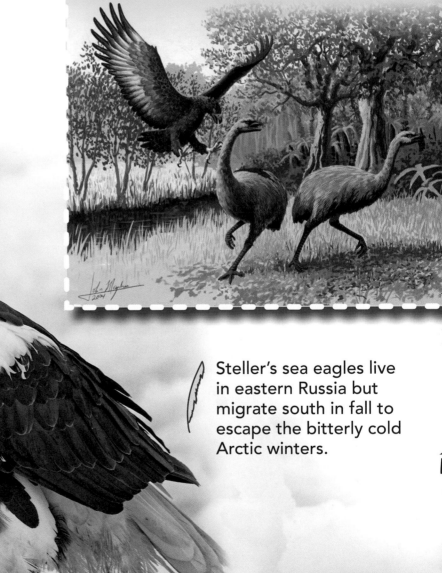

Steller's sea eagles live in eastern Russia but migrate south in fall to escape the bitterly cold Arctic winters.

The Bald Eagle

The bald eagle is a type of eagle found in North America. With a wingspan of 7.5 feet (2.3 m) and a body length of about 3.3 feet (1 m), it is not the largest eagle in North America, but it is the best known.

White head

Yellow hooked beak

Dark brown feathers

Dangerous Times

When Europeans first arrived in North America, there were about half a million bald eagles. The bald eagle was chosen to be the country's emblem because people thought it represented strength and freedom. Sadly, over the next 150 years, most of the eagles were killed because people thought they hunted their farm animals.

The bald eagle isn't really bald. Its name comes from "piebald," which means having patches of white on brown or black.

A New Threat

In 1940, the U.S. government passed a law to protect the remaining birds. Although the eagles increased in number, they were threatened again by the use of the **pesticide** DDT, which poisoned the adult birds. In 1967, the bald eagle was declared an **endangered** species.

Success Story

The work of **conservation** organizations has paid off, and now the number of bald eagles has crept back to about 70,000. The bald eagle is no longer considered to be an endangered species. About half of the eagles live in Alaska, 20,000 live in Canada, and the remaining birds are found across the rest of the United States, from Oregon to Florida.

These bald eagles in Alaska are fighting over food.

High Fliers

Eagles are expert fliers. Their powerful wings take them high into the sky where they can look down and search for prey.

Large But Light

Eagles have long, broad wings that are covered in feathers. The wings are incredibly strong, but they are light because the bones are hollow. The wings of a bald eagle, for example, have a span of more than 6.5 feet (2 m), but weigh just 2.2 pounds (1 kg). The feathers are strong, too. The longest wing feathers are called the primary flight feathers and may be 12 inches (30 cm) or more in length.

Primary flight feathers

An eagle has broad wings, with long flight feathers. The longest feathers are at the wing tips.

Soaring Flight

When an eagle takes off, it flaps its wings to gain height. Then it tries to find a column of rising air that carries it effortlessly for hundreds of feet into the sky. The eagle then glides down again, at speeds of 31 miles (50 km) per hour or more. By using these currents, known as **thermals**, eagles can cover long distances and rarely have to flap their wings.

Once an eagle has spotted prey on the ground, it has to swoop down quickly before the prey can escape. The eagle folds its wings back to create a smaller wing. This allows it to dive to the ground far more quickly.

Folded wings increase the eagle's speed as it swoops to the ground.

AERIAL ACROBAT

The bateleur eagle gets its name from a French word that means "tightrope walker." As the bateleur flies along, it tilts its wings from side to side, just like a tightrope walker trying to balance. It can perform twists, turns, and even somersaults in the air.

Tail feathers for balance

Feathers spread out like fingers, so air flows smoothly over the wing

A bateleur eagle may fly up to 186 miles (300 km) each day in search of food.

13

Eagle Food

Eagles are **carnivores**, which means they eat other animals. Bald eagles feast on fish, ducks, and small **mammals**. Snake eagles like to eat frogs, lizards, and snakes. Buzzard eagles, such as the harpy, feed on small monkeys, birds, and lizards.

Choosing Prey

Eagles usually hunt small prey so they can lift the animal off the ground and fly to the safety of a perch. But the largest eagles, such as the harpy and sea eagle, can carry weights of up to 6.5 pounds (3 kg). When a large creature is killed, the eagle rips it apart on the ground and carries the pieces away. Many eagles are scavengers, too, particularly in winter when food may be scarce.

Eagles fly to their favorite perch to eat their prey. They grip the perch with one foot while they rip off lumps of meat with the talons of the other.

Storing Food

Eagles have a pouch in their throat called a crop that they use to store food. Inside the crop, the food is churned around so the meat is separated from other parts, such as bones, fur, and feathers. The eagle spits out these inedible parts, which are mixed with slimy mucus to form a pellet. Scientists learn a lot about an eagle's diet by examining these pellets.

Short-toed eagle is a type of snake eagle

Eagle eats snakes and swallows them whole

A DIET OF SNAKES

The snake eagle loves to eat snakes— even **poisonous** ones. When it spots a snake from its tree perch, it dives down and catches the snake behind the head. When it flies back to the tree, it swallows the snake whole, just like a piece of spaghetti!

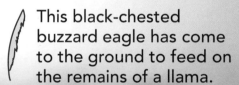

This black-chested buzzard eagle has come to the ground to feed on the remains of a llama.

On the Hunt

Most birds of prey, including eagles, hunt during the day because they rely on their sight to find prey. Eagles have found different ways of tracking down a tasty meal.

Perching and Swooping

Some eagles sit on a tall tree or a steep cliff and watch for prey animals to move on the ground. Others, such as the golden eagle, soar into the sky and hunt from above. When an eagle sees movement, it swoops down at great speed to catch its prey on the ground. Sea eagles drag their talons through the water to catch fish. Sometimes, golden eagles are seen flying close to the ground, so they can catch their prey by surprise.

 This black-chested harrier eagle is keeping an eye out for its next meal.

Razor-sharp hooked talons and rough bumps on the toes help the eagle grip its prey.

SUPER SWIMMERS

The bald eagle usually snatches fish from the surface of a river, a lake, or the ocean. But it can swim underwater to catch fish, too. The eagle may even be dragged into the water by a large fish. When this happens, the eagle uses its wings to swim to shore. It has to dry its feathers before it can fly away.

Stealing Food

Another way to get food is to steal it from other birds of prey. Often an eagle will chase another bird that has food in its talons. The chased bird is bullied into dropping its food, which is caught in midair by the eagle. If the chased bird does not release the food, it may be attacked.

An African fish eagle fights with a maribou stork for some meat.

The Golden Eagle

There are many stories of golden eagles carrying off sheep, mountain goats, and even human babies. Although they are large birds, with a wingspan of 6.5 feet (2 m) or more, golden eagles cannot lift large animals from the ground.

Varied Diet

Golden eagles like to eat rabbits and other small mammals, such as prairie dogs, small birds, grouse, and duck. They scavenge on animal remains, and if they are hungry they will attack other **predators**, such as owls and hawks. Some pairs of golden eagles work together on the hunt, with one eagle driving the prey toward their partner.

The golden eagle has a wingspan of about 6.5 feet (2 m), a body length of 3.3 feet (1 m), and weighs up to 15 pounds (7 kg).

Golden feathers on neck and head

Long wingspan makes flying easier

Fine Feathers

The golden eagle is a booted eagle with feathers all the way down to its legs and toes. It is mainly found in the mountains of North America and across Europe and Asia. Years ago, it lived in many more places, such as North Africa and Japan.

Golden Hunter

In some Central Asian countries, such as Kazakhstan and Mongolia, the golden eagle is popular with **falconers** who train the eagle to hunt wolves and foxes. They call the bird the *berkut*. Wolves are difficult to kill, so the falconer uses the eagle to find a wolf and knock it to the ground so the falconer can kill it.

Golden eagles have feathers down to their toes, just like a pair of "boots."

These Kazakh falconers hunt on horseback, releasing their golden eagles to bring down wolves and foxes.

19

Building Nests

Eagles do not hunt just anywhere. They live in a **home range** (or territory) in which they nest and find food. They guard their home range from other eagles, chasing away any that come too close.

High Living

The correct name for an eagle's nest is an aerie. It is usually built in places that are out of reach, such as a cliff ledge or the top of a tall tree. In the Karoo Desert of South Africa, martial eagles build their nests on electric towers.

An eagle's nest is enormous. It looks like a huge jumble of twigs, but in fact, each twig has been carefully placed in position to keep the nest stable. When an eagle has finished building its nest, it lines it with softer material such as leaves, rushes, and grass.

An aerie can be more than 3.3 feet (1 m) across and up to 6.5 feet (2 m) deep.

Partners for Life

Eagles mate for life. Each year, an eagle pair returns to the same nest site. As they make repairs and add new twigs, their nest gets gradually larger. This means that the largest nests are usually home to the oldest eagles. If one of the eagles dies, the surviving eagle chooses a new partner for life.

Scientists think that the grasses lining an eagle's nest reduce smells and make the nest cooler for eagle chicks.

RECORD-BREAKER

The largest known bald eagle nest was found in Florida. It was almost 9 feet (2.7 m) wide and 20 feet (6 m) deep. It was estimated to weigh a massive 2.2 tons (2 metric tons) and had been used for many years.

Young Eagles

The female eagle lays up to three eggs over a period of about a week. The eggs are then **incubated** for up to 60 days. Most male and female eagles share the incubating duties, with one sitting on the nest while the other hunts for food.

Firstborn

The eggs do not hatch at the same time. The egg that was laid first is the first to hatch. This chick has the advantage of being a few days older than its siblings, so it is larger and stronger. At meal times, it pushes the other chicks out of the way. Sometimes, smaller chicks die because they don't get enough to eat. This sounds cruel, but it is the only way of making sure that one healthy chick survives.

A mother uses her beak to feed her chicks with meat so they can grow healthy and strong.

DANGEROUS TALONS

When an eagle is in the nest with young chicks, it keeps its talons curled up like a ball, to keep the razor-sharp edges away from its babies.

Leaving the Nest

The young chicks are covered in fluffy white feathers and don't look like eagles at all! They get their proper feathers at about 11 weeks old, when they begin to take their first short flights from the nest. Some young eagles are ready to live on their own when they are about five months old, but young harpy eagles stay with their parents for as long as two years.

Young eagles have different feathers than their parents. They grow a new set of feathers every year as they get older.

Eagles Under Threat

Eagles are disappearing all over the world. Sadly, a few are very close to becoming extinct—such as the Madagascar fish eagle and the Philippine eagle.

Poisonous Pesticide

During the 1950s and 1960s, a pesticide called DDT was sprayed onto crops to kill pests such as insects. The poisoned insects were eaten by small birds, which in turn were eaten by eagles. The poison built up in the eagles' bodies and killed them. DDT is now banned in many countries, but other poisons are still used.

Saving Eagles

There are many ways that we can help to save eagles. One way is to prevent their habitat from disappearing. In Brazil, for example, jungle trees are being cut down, which is threatening the harpy eagle. Another way is to protect eagle nests and to prevent people from stealing the eggs.

Around the world, forests are being cut down for building projects. Many eagles are losing their forest homes.

Eagle Watch

Nowadays, many people travel long distances to watch eagles—sea eagles in Japan, bald eagles in Alaska, and golden eagles in Scotland are all popular tourist attractions. This brings money into an area that can be used for conserving more eagles. The money also helps to create jobs and makes the local people even more determined to protect their eagles.

These men are hoping to catch a glimpse of a nesting eagle.

Sometimes, rare eagles are kept in zoos where there are breeding programs. This Philippine eagle lives in an eagle center in the Philippines.

The Harpy Eagle

Harpy eagles are one of the largest and most powerful of the eagles, but despite their strength and size, they are also the most threatened.

Vanishing Homes

The main threat to harpy eagles is the loss of their jungle homes due to **deforestation**. A pair of harpy eagles needs a massive 8 square miles (20 sq km) of jungle, so only a few birds live in a large area. In 2002, scientists had found fewer than 50 harpy nests in the Central and South American jungles. Harpy eagles are also shot because people are afraid of them, or want to use their feathers.

The fierce-looking harpy eagle has a warlike headdress of spiky feathers. It is larger than the golden eagle.

Skilled Fliers

The harpy eagle has adapted perfectly to life among the trees. Their broad, short wings and square tail help them to rise almost vertically, like a harrier jump jet, and steer between the trees as they fly looking for prey. They chase macaws and other birds, and snatch lizards, monkeys, and even sloths from the branches.

A harpy eagle is big enough to attack a sloth climbing among the trees.

Breeding Success

A breeding program for harpy eagles in Panama, Central America, has been a great success. Over the last few years, 30 harpy eagles have been released back into the jungles of Panama and Belize.

Young harpy eagles stay with their parents for up to two years, so it takes a long time for the number of eagles to increase.

Facts and Records

Eagles have earned their reputation as king of the birds. With their massive wings, these magnificent creatures are amazing in many ways.

Largest and Smallest

- The largest eagle is the Philippine eagle, with a wingspan of more than 6.5 feet (2 m).

- The smallest eagle is the ornate hawk-eagle, with wings just under 4 feet (1.2 m) across.

- Female eagles are much larger than the males.

The ornate hawk-eagle weighs just over 2.2 pounds (1 kg).

Body Facts

- Eagles have a third eyelid that moves across the surface of the eye every few seconds, keeping it clear of dirt and dust.

- As part of their courtship, a pair of bald eagles lock their talons together and whirl around in the air.

Did You Know?

- Golden eagles have been known to eat turtles in Greece. They drop them from a great height onto rocks to break their shells.

- The white-tailed sea eagle became extinct in Britain during the nineteenth century but has been reintroduced to Scotland.

Record-Breakers

- The extinct Haast's eagle had a wingspan of more than 8.5 feet (2.6 m) and weighed a massive 44 pounds (20 kg).

- The martial eagle is the largest eagle in Africa. It has been known to kill animals that are ten times its own weight, such as impalas.

- The wedge-tailed eagle of Australia rises on thermals to heights of more than 1.2 miles (2 km) above the ground.

The martial eagle is an aggressive predator.

Names and Numbers

- Birds of prey such as eagles are often called raptors. This word comes from the Latin word *rapere*, which means "to grip."

- The golden eagle has been called the "War Bird" because Native Americans used eagle feathers to decorate the headdresses they wore into battle.

- Eagles live for 20–30 years in the wild. They live for more than 40 years in captivity.

- Up to 40 percent of young bald eagles do not survive their first flight.

Special Features

- The young bateleur eagle has extra-long wing feathers to help it learn to fly—like training wheels on a bike. As the eagle gets older, its wing feathers get shorter.

- The color of the bateleur's face and feet ranges from pale orange to bright red, depending on its mood. The males have particularly red faces and feet during the breeding season.

Glossary

camouflage
the colors and patterns on an animal's skin, fur, or feathers that help it blend with its surroundings so that it is hard to see

carnivore
an animal that eats meat

coat of arms
a design that represents a family, city, or country

conservation
the protection of natural habitats, plants, and animals

deforestation
the cutting down of trees for wood to use, or to clear an area for building or agriculture

endangered
at risk of becoming extinct

extinct
no longer in existence, having died out

falconer
someone who keeps or trains birds of prey, such as eagles, to hunt other animals

habitat
a particular place where plants and animals live, such as a tropical forest or a snowy region

home range
the whole area in which an animal lives and looks for food

incubate
to keep warm—parent eagles keep their eggs warm until they hatch

jungle
dense forest found in tropical parts of the world

mammal
an animal that feeds its young on milk and has hair on its body

migrate
to make the same journey at the same time each year

native
people, plants, or animals that come from a particular place and have not traveled there

pesticide
a substance
that kills
pests (such as
insects) that
damage crops

poisonous
harmful

predator
an animal that
hunts others
for food

prey
an animal that is
eaten for food
by another

scavenge
to search for
leftover food and
animal remains

species
a particular type
of animal, such
as an eagle

thermal
a current of rising
warm air

tropical
an area or climate
that is warm and
often wet, close
to the equator
(the imaginary
line around the
Earth's middle)

Index

Web Finder

Bald Eagle Kid's Page
www.eaglestock.com/kidspage.htm
Find out about bald eagles and how you can help to save them.

American Eagle Foundation
www.eagles.org/all
Learn about the foundation's efforts to save the bald eagle.

Avian Web
www.avianweb.com/eagles.htm
Learn about different types of eagles around the world.

RSPB Kids
www.rspb.org.uk/youth
Find out about birds of prey, including the white-tailed eagle.

National Geographic
http://animals.nationalgeographic.com/animals/birds
Find out about different types of eagles, such as the bald, golden, and Steller's sea eagle, watch videos, and hear their cries.